READ A STORY - FIND A JOB

GETTING JOBS AS EASY AS READING STORIES

I0491040

RAM GEE

An imprint of Notion Press

XpressPublishing
An Imprint of Notion Press

No.8, 3rd Cross Street,CIT Colony,
Mylapore, Chennai, Tamil Nadu-600004

ISBN 978-1-64919-389-6

I am deeply indebted to my family and friends who inculcated the habit of reading a variety of books,

not just textbooks.

Special thanks to Sunil and Sriram, my childhood friend and my brother.

Contents

Contents

Preface

One day i was with my friends in a coffeeshop, we were recollecting our past childhood memories,

when the waiter comes along and asks "some more coffee, Sir", i say yes, as he was pouring it kind of dropped it onto my trousers, i stared and gave him a glance, said "that's ok" it happens.

Life is full of incidents big and small, not all things whether hardship, happiness, enjoyment, etc will last forever, they will have commas, fullstops and journey of life will go on.

Acknowledgements

I wish to thank the entire team at Notion Publishers for getting my book published with such an ease,

as much as this book title "read a story - find a job"

thank you all at Notion.

Prologue

HUMANS BY CHANGING THE INNER ATTITUDES OF THEIR MINDS,
CAN CHANGE THE OUTER ASPECTS OF THEIR LIVES"

CHAPTER ONE

SUCCESS OR FAILURE

Five pilgrims on a spiritual journey arrived at a Dharamshala in the foothills of himalayas.

There was only a watchman and there was one room but the watchman warned that there could be a snake......

one of them overcame his fear and decided to check the room. On entering, he didnt find a snake but

a rope, which resembled a snake.

This man took the room and slept soundly, while others left searching for a better place.

We fear failure, becuase we fear criticism, rejection, etc.

The truth is that anyone who has been successful has failed at some stage of their life.

From failure comes knowledge of what works and what doesn't. From failure comes knowledge of one's strenghts and weaknesses.

Also success or failure is a relative term: what one perceives as extraordinary success may be an ordinary accomplishment to another.

CHAPTER TWO

SEARCHING FOR A JOB?

Are you ready to start a search for an online position? Here's to find your first work-from-home job, and how to get started looking for jobs you can work online. This book gives tips and tricks to finding an online job that will help you in real job opportunities, show you where and how to look for well-paid remote jobs you can do on your schedule and work from wherever you want, and provide advice on how to search smartly and get hired.

There's a very simple rule when it comes to looking for work at home jobs. Don't pay a fee - for anything. In most cases, you shouldn't pay for job listings, you shouldn't pay to apply for jobs, and you shouldn't pay a fee to get on the payroll. Companies pay you a salary. You don't pay them to hire you. Here's more information on no fee work at home jobs.

There are legitimate work from home jobs available. However, before you apply, it's important to carefully research the company to make sure the job is legitimate and not a scam designed to take your money or your personal information.

Read a story and find a job is all about making an online job as easy as reading a story.

Each chapter after a story gives you complete details on how to get an online job, resources, contact details and even website address.

CHAPTER THREE

BELIEF IN GOD

There was a christian lady who lived next door to an athiest. Everdyday, when the lady
prayed, the athiest found this annoying and one day went to her house, said, "lady, why do you pray all the time? dont you know there is no god?"

But the lady kept on praying, one day she ran out of groceries, as usual the athiest heard her saying no groceries, he thought he will teach her a lesson.

He went to the grocery store, bought a whole bunch of groceries, took them to her house, dropped them off on the front porch, rang the bell and hid in the bushes to see what she would do.

when she opened the door and saw the groceries, she began to praise the lord with all her heart, jumping, singing in joy.

The atheist then jumped out of the bushes and told her, "you old crazy lady, god didnt but those groceries, i bought those groceries."

She replied " i knew the lord would provide me with groceries, but i didnt know he was going to make the devil pay for them".

CHAPTER FOUR

ONLINE SURVEY JOBS

If you are not a specialist in anything and want a simple chore then this online survey jobs is the best

Online Survey Jobs

Online surveys are a great way to make Rs 10,000 to Rs 20,000 per month working just 2 – 3 hours a day online.

Usually surveys are conducted by various companies to ascertain what consumers think of their product and services. Companies want to know whether they liked their product or not.

Hence, they need people like you to share your opinion with them. These companies outsource their work to various third parties and these parties provide you survey jobs where you need to fill a form containing simple questionnaires.

You need to answer these questions.

Each form has few questions in them that can be finished in 5 – 20 minutes depending upon number of questions being asked. That's it!

But there is one caveat, finding a genuine online survey sites could be a daunting task. But don't worry, we did it for you!

On your part do thorough research and background check of each site before joining this type of online work.

1. https://www.triaba.in/

2.https://www.mobrog.com/en-in/

3. https://www.awwro.com/

4. https://indiaearns.in/online-survey-jobs/

CHAPTER FIVE

THE PAIN OF LIFE IS PURE SALT

Once a young man came to a revered teacher, who was seated under a tree near a beautiful lake,

asked for solutions for his unhappiness.

After few minutes of cooncersation the old master kindly instructed the young man to put a handful of salt in a glass of water and then to drink a few sips, " how does it taste?" the teacher asked.

"Awful" said the young man.

The teacher chuckled and then asked the young man to take a handful of salt and put it in the lake.

the two walked in silence to the nearby lake and when the young man swirled his handful of salt into he the lake, the teacher told him, " now drink a few sips from the lake"'

As the water dripped down the young man's chin, the teacher asked him again, "how does it taste?"

"good!" replied the young man.

"did you taste the salt?" asked the teacher. No, said the young man.

The Teacher sat beside the young man, took his hands, and said, the pain of life is pure salt; no more, no less.

So when you are in pain, the only thing you can do is to enlarge your sense of things, you have to stop being a glass.

Instead become a lake, you can become a lake by broadening your heart, when you stop looking at your miseries, your troubles.

Look at blessings that god has given you. then your miseries will disappear into the lake.

CHAPTER SIX

ONLINE SELLING JOBS

Online Selling Jobs

I personally know many of the people who are selling different products on sites like Amazon India, eBay India etc. and earning anywhere between Rs. 20,000 to Rs.1,00,000 per month.

It's not a difficult job. Anyone can become an online seller and make a profit. You can do part time or full time.

Here are the steps to start selling online-

Look for some local dealers or distributors where you can find some hot selling products at lowest price.

Signup as seller on Amazon, Flipkart, eBay or these 60 online shopping sites.

List all your products on the sites with the selling price.

Receive orders

Deliver the products through courier

Make profit

People always check reviews before they order any product on shopping sites. Try to provide the best services to your buyers so that they can write good reviews about you & your products.

This will help you increase the sales.

CHAPTER SEVEN

LOOK AT YOUR HORIZON

One day a father and his young son took a trip to a village with the purpose to show his son how poor people can be.

they spent a day and a night in the farm, when they got back from the trip, the father asked his son

"how was the trip?" very good, dad! "did you see how poor people can be?" yeah replied the son.

"what did you learn?" said the father.

the son answered, "i saw that we have a dog at home, and they have plenty, we have a pool and they have a creek that has no end, we have imported lamps and they have stars, we have a patio and they have whole sky. when the son was finishing, his father was speechless.

His son added, " thanks, dad, for showing me how poor we are!"

isnt it true it all depends on the way you look at things?

If you have love, family, friends, health and a positive attittude, you got everything!

CHAPTER EIGHT

DATA ENTRY JOBS

Data Entry Jobs

There is nothing new about online Data Entry Jobs. You have being listening about them since you discovered Internet.

Data entry jobs could be

Copy and Paste Work

Formatting files using MS Word and MS Excel

Converting clients digital/Image files into Word Documents

Tracking inventory and shipments by entering data into Excel

So they are plenty. Finding a genuine Data Entry job which pays you on time regularly could be very challenging but we made it easier for you.

2 things you must remember while searching data entry work online.

Never pay a fee for joining a data entry company.

Secondly do a thorough background check of the company you would like to work for. Go to their Contact Us page, see if phone number is given, dial them and ask every small detail about the company. In fact pay a visit to their office and talk in person.

Earning Rs 10,000 – Rs 25,000 per month wouldn't be that difficult with this online work. Go ahead!

1. https://www.aasaanjobs.com/s/data-entry-operator-jobs/

2. https://worknhire.com/data_entry_jobs/

3. hiresine.com mostly pays in us dollars

4. workindia.in

CHAPTER NINE

BREAK THE SILENCE

A man and his wife were having some problems at home and were giving each other a silent
treatment. Suddenly, the man realized that the next day, he would need his wife to wake him at 5AM
for an early morning flight.

Not wanting to be the first to break silence, he wrote on a piece of paper, "please wake me up at 5AM".

He left it where he knew she would find it. The next day morning, the man woke up only to discover that it was 9AM and he missed the flight.

Furious, he was about to go and see why his wife hadnt woke him up, when he noticed a piece of paper by his bedside, the paper said, " It is 5AM, wake up".

CHAPTER TEN

COOKING JOBS

IF YOU A GOOD COOK, YOU CAN DISH OUT VARIETY OF DISHES, THEN YOU MIGHT TRY

VARIOUS JOBS ONLINE BY BEING A PART TIME COOK FOR NUMEROUS COMPANIES DELIVERING HOME MADE FOODS.

OR BETTER STARTING YOUR OWN HOME MADE FOOD WITH A SIMPLE WEBSITE AND A DELIVERY BOY TO START WITH.

THE DEMAND FOR HOME MADE FOODS IS INCREASING IN INDIA, CATERING TO FUNCTIONS AND WEDDINGS IS ANOTHER OUTLET THAT YOU COULD EASILY VENTURE INTO SLOWLY.

1. https://www.watscooking.com/
2. https://www.authenticook.com/
3. https://www.masalabox.com/
4. box8 app & https://www.ootabox.com/

CHAPTER ELEVEN

ANT AND THE FEATHER

One morning i was watching a tiny ant carry a huge feather, several times it was confronted by obstacles in its path and after a momentary pause it would make the necessary detour.

At one point the ant had to negotiate a crack in the concrete about 2mm wide, after brief contemplation the ant laid the feather over the crack, went across it and picked up the feather on the other side then continued.

After sometime the ant reached its destination, a small hole that was the entrance to its underground home. And it was here that the ant finally met its match, how could that large feather possibly fit down small hole.

Of course, it couldnt. So the ant, after all the trouble and ecercising great ingenuity, overcoming obstacles, just abandoned the feather.

The feather was nothing more than burden, isnt life like that sometimes we carry the burden of worries, pain all for nothing.

CHAPTER TWELVE

BLOGGING

Blogging

So if you are thinking what this hell blogging is, then I will explain you in layman language "just create a website & publish some useful content in your website on regular basis". or post some artcles and interesting clips on bloggers post.

You create a website, start posting articles on a particular topic (your favourite topic) & start earning money.

so how can someone make money by creating a site & simply posting content.

There are various ways to make money from your blog. Google AdSense & affiliate marketing are the most popular.

My favourite is Google AdSense

Yes, I am serious.

You apply for AdSense account-> Google places the ads on your blog->Your visitor clicks on these ads->You earn money

Here are the exact steps to make money from a blog-

You start a blog

Write high quality posts on your blog

Get traffic by promoting on other sites or search engine (SEO)

Use Adsense ads or affiliate programs on your blog

Earn lots of money

Few Sites for blogging:

1. Blogger
2. Quora
3. Wordpress
4. roon
5.SETT
6.livejournal.com

CHAPTER THIRTEEN

MARK TWAIN AND THE BISHOP

The Famous American writer, Mark Twain once attended a church service. The Bishop delivered
an extempore (not prepared) sermon. After the sermon, he asked Mark Twain "sir, How did you find my sermon?" Mark Twain his usual satirical way said: " Sir, your sermon was good, of course but, every word
you spoke is already in this book with me!".

The bishop wondered how every word he spoke extempore had already been in a book. So he said, "sir, may i see the book?"

Mark Twain took the oxford dictionary from his bag and handed it to the bishop.

CHAPTER FOURTEEN

ONLINE WRITING JOBS

Those of you who can write then there is no better online job than writing. You can become a freelance writer through various freelance sites mentioned here.

If you know there are thousands of freelance writers around the world who are earning a decent income writing online.

In India, you can easily earn up to Rs 35,000 – Rs 40,000 per month writing online.

Freelance writing can be

Web content writing

Ghost writing,

Technical writing,

Business writing,

Copywriting,

Newspaper writing etc

Editing and Proofreading

If you are a writer who can write simple English with no grammatical error then there is no dearth of writing jobs online.

1. WRITERBAY

CHAPTER FIFTEEN

HITTING THE NAIL

There was a little boy who had a bad temper, his father gave him a bag of nails and told him that every time he lost his temper, he must hammer a nail into the fence.

The first day the boy had driven 37 nails, over the next few weeks as he learned to control his anger the number of nails hammered daily, gradually declined. He discovered that it was easier to control his temper than to drive those nails into the fence. Finally the day came when the boy didnt lose his temper at all. He told his father about it and the father suggested that the boy now pull out one nail for each day that he was able to control his temper.

The days passed and the young boy was finally able to tell his father that all the nails were gone. The father took his son by the hand and led him to the fence. He said "you have done well, my son, but look at the holes in the fence. The fence will never be the same again. When you say things in anger, they leave a scar just like this one."

You can hurt a man and draw it out, it wont matter how many times you say sorry, the wound is still there.

CHAPTER SIXTEEN

DIGITAL MARKETING JOBS

Digital Marketing Jobs

Unlike previous few online jobs, digital marketing are quite new to scene. In last 5 years, they have become quite popular especially among younger generation.

There are two great things about digital marketing jobs, first one is you can do online and second is remuneration, it's really great.

Here are some of the digital marketing jobs

SEO, SEM (Search Engine Marketing)

Content and Video Marketing

Email Marketing

E-Commerce Marketing

Web Analytics

Mobile Advertising etc.

Right now SEO jobs are in very high demand and selling like hot cake. SEO experts those who know their work are earning decent money working online.

Digital marketing can easily pay you Rs 10,000 – Rs 35,000 per month.

13. Social Media Jobs

If you find digital marketing jobs tough then you can look out for social media jobs. Here are some of them.

1. Virtual Assistant: As a virtual assistant you will assist managers and executives online with tasks like organizing files, answering phones, managing files etc. Knowledge of MS Office, Google Apps, Dropbox is very important.

2. Social Media Managers and Moderators: Social media managers and moderators manage social media platforms like Facebook, Twitter, YouTube and other online forums/ groups. You assist visitors, respond their comments and feedback, delete inappropriate comments and manage threads.

3. Chat/Email Support: Instead of calling from phone, you will reach out customers through online chat and email. You will be paid for assisting people online by chatting and email support.

You are paid well for each online job and earn Rs 12,000 to Rs 25,000 a month depending upon your experience. You can find social media jobs on job portals like Naukri and Indeed.

CHAPTER SEVENTEEN

BELIEVING STRANGERS

King Krishnadevaraya loved horses and had the best collection of horse breeds in the Kingdom. Well, one day, a trader came to the King and told him that he had brought with him a horse of the best breed in Arabia.

He invited the King to inspect the horse. King Krishnadevaraya loved the horse; so the trader said that the King could buy this one and that he had two more like this one, back in Arabia that he would go back to get. The King loved the horse so much that he had to have the other two as well. He paid the trader 5000 gold coins in advance. The trader promised that he would return within two days with the other horses.

Two days turned into two weeks, and still, there was no sign of the trader and the two horses. One evening, to ease his mind, the King went on a stroll in his garden. There he spotted Tenali Raman writing down something on a piece of paper. Curious, the King asked Tenali what he was jotting down.

Tenali Raman was hesitant, but after further questioning, he showed the King the paper. On the paper was a list of names, the King's being at the top of the list.

Tenali said these were the names of the biggest fools in the Vijayanagara Kingdom!

As expected, the King was furious that his name was at the top and asked Tenali Raman for an explanation. Tenali referred to the horse story, saying the King was a fool to believe that the trader, a stranger, would return after receiving 5000 gold coins.

Countering his argument, the King then asked, what happens if/when the trader does come back? In true Tenali humour, he replied saying, in that case, the trader would be a bigger fool, and his name would replace the King's on the list!

Moral – Don't believe strangers blindly.

CHAPTER EIGHTEEN

ONLINE TRANSCRIPTION JOBS

Online Transcription Jobs

Usually people confuse transcription jobs with data entry work. Indeed, they both are quite different. In transcription you listen to audio/video files and convert them into a word file.

Transcription services are often given for medical or legal (mainly medical) purposes. The job is quite demanding because you need total control over medical and legal jargons.

You must have some prior experience transcribing audio/video files. Moreover, your typing speed must be over 60 words per minute.

However, you are paid well as a transcriptionist. A transcriptionist makes 4 to5 times more than a data entry worker.

In India, you can find genuine online transcription jobs if you are willing to do some research.

Salary of a transcriptionist is really good.

1. https://gotranscript.com/indian-transcription-and-translation-services

2. https://www.voxtab.com/careers.htm

3. https://www.truelancer.com/transcription-freelancers-in-india

4. https://www.upwork.com/freelance-jobs/medical-transcription/

CHAPTER NINETEEN

TENALI RAMAN AND THE KING

In the King's court, there was a very orthodox teacher named Tathacharya who belonged to the Vaishnavite sect. He looked down on other people, especially the Smarthas – covering his face with a cloth whenever he saw people from this and other sects.

Fed up of this behaviour, the King and other courtiers went to Tenali Raman for his help. After listening to everyone's complaints about the royal teacher, Tenali Raman went to Tathacharya's house. Upon seeing Tenali, the teacher covered his face. Seeing this, Tenali asked him why he did that. He explained that Smarthas were sinners and to look upon the face of a sinner meant that he would be turned into a donkey in his next life. That's when an idea struck Tenali!

One day, Tenali, the King, Tathacharya and the other courtiers went on a picnic together. As they were returning from their picnic, Tenali spotted some donkeys. He immediately ran up to them and started saluting them. Puzzled, the King asked Tenali why he was saluting the donkeys. Tenali then explained that he was paying his respects to Tathacharya's ancestors, who had become donkeys after looking at the faces of Smarthas.

Tathacharya understood Tenali's harmless behaviour, and from that day forward, never covered his face again.

Moral – Don't judge people on their ETHNICITY

CHAPTER TWENTY

ONLINE TUTORING JOBS

Online Tutoring

Online tutoring jobs give you an opportunity to make some extra money right from your home. Especially, if you are a college graduate.

The best thing about online tutoring is you can teach students on part time basis. Just 2 to 3 hours a day is enough for earning Rs 10,000 – Rs 20,000 a month.

You must have some prior experience with teaching or tutoring.

You can choose a subject of your interest and conduct an hour long session through video calling. Some of the subjects you can choose from are

Math

Physics

History

Finance

Economics

Accounting

Languages like English, German, Japanese etc

Literature

Law

Sociology etc.
So join now-
https://tutorindia.net/Tutor_Jobs
https://www.vedantu.com/become-a-teacher

CHAPTER TWENTY-ONE

STORY OF SUN AND THE WIND

1. The Wind and the Sun

There was once an argument between the wind and the sun about who was stronger than the other. They argued for a long time but neither of them emerged the winner. It wasn't too long before they spotted a man walking on the road. Looking at the man wearing a coat, an idea struck them both.

They challenged each other that the one who succeeded in removing the coat from the man's back was the strongest.

The wind volunteered to try first. It began to blow hard, raising gusts of air and making it harder for the man to take a step further.

But, the man clutched his coat tight around him and resumed walking with great difficulty.

The wind continued blowing harder and harder, but the man held on to his coat tighter and tighter. And continued his journey forward. Finally, the wind was exhausted and gave up. His efforts had been futile.

It was now the turn of the sun. He looked at the man and began to gently shine upon the path the man was walking on.

The man looked up at the sky – surprised at the change in weather.

The sun did not spend much energy, neither did he apply any effort. He just continued shining upon the man's head gently.

Soon the man was huffing and puffing, and sweating profusely.

Unable to bear the rising heat, the man finally took off his coat and headed to a nearby tree to rest for a while under its shade.

Moral: Sometimes gentle persuasion is mightier than the strongest force.

CHAPTER TWENTY-TWO

SELLING PHOTOS JOBS

Earn Money Selling photos

Sell photos taken from your smartphone and get paid for each single photograph. You can use your photography and selfie taking skills to make some money from this online job.

You have to take professional looking photos from your smartphone and sell to websites like Shutterstock, Fotolia, iStock Photo online.

You don't even have to buy a camera because today every smartphone comes with a very powerful camera.

Each photo can pay you anything $0.25 to $30 depending upon the quality of the photo.

However, you must remember taking photos are not as easy as taking selfies. Hence, photos must look professional in order to sell them.

You just have to download and install apps like Foap, Twenty20 etc. onto your phone and start selling photos.

CHAPTER TWENTY-THREE

THE ANT AND THE DOVE

The Ant and The Dove – An Aesop's Fable

Once an ant was drinking water at the bank of a river. Suddenly a huge wave lapped at him and he fell into the water. The tiny could not swim against the strong current and reach the shore.

A dove sitting in a tree near the river bank saw the ant struggling in the water. The dove plucked a leaf from the tree, flew over to where the ant was and threw the leaf into the water.

The ant climbed on to the leaf and floated safely to the river bank.

Shortly afterwards, a bird-catcher came to the river to catch birds. He laid out a net and started spreading twigs and grains on the net.

The ant watched the bird-catcher and understood his intentions. He crawled up to the bird-catcher and stung him the foot.

The bird-catcher cried out loudly in pain. The dove heard the bird-catcher and flew away to safety.

Moral: A good deed never goes unnoticed.

CHAPTER TWENTY-FOUR

STOCK MARKET & VIRTUAL TRADING

Stock Trading

Last but not the least is stock trading. You can trade stocks online and earn money. Intraday traders earn huge profits trading not just stocks but commodities and currencies too.

Although you can make great money trading however it is not for everyone because a lot of risk is involved here.

If you have a good knowledge about the markets then you can create an account with a broker and get started.

Everything is done online on your laptop. You buy shares for low price and sell them high. Whether you earn money or lose it, the amount is credited/debited to your account online.

Moneycontrol website offers Moneybhai. It is a free virtual trading platform where you'll get **Rs 1 crore virtual cash** on registration which you can use to invest in shares, commodities, mutual funds, or fixed deposits on the platform.

At Moneybhai, you can also compete with fellow Indian traders by joining different leagues. There's also a free forum on this website where you can ask your queries or participate in the on-going discussion threads.

2. TrakInvest

Website— http://www.trakinvest.com/
https://tradebrains.in/get/zerodha/

TrakInvest is a global trading platform that helps you to learn, develop and improve your investing skills. Currently, it provides a curated market data and news from 10 exchanges. It also offers beginners' guides and videos, certification courses designed by industry experts and simulations for competing for rewards.

At TrakInvest, you can also track other traders and dig deeper into their trading activity (portfolio) where you can replicate their trades using the 'Copy Trade' facility. Overall, TrakInvest provides a simple and friendly platform for 'Social' virtual trading for beginners.

3. Dalal Street

Website: https://www.dsij.in/Stock-Market-Challenge

Dalal Street Investment Journal (DSIJ) popular virtual stock trading platform in India which helps you to understand the different trading nuances and to test your investment strategies.

On registration, you'll get virtual cash of Rs 1,000,0000 to create your portfolio. At DSIJ, you can also discuss strategies with like-minded participants in the discussion group.

New to stocks? Confused where to begin? Here's an amazing online course for beginners: 'HOW TO PICK WINNING STOCKS?' This course is currently available at a discount.

Bonus: Investopedia stock simulator

Website: https://www.investopedia.com/simulator/

This is my favorite stock simulator.

Investopedia provides a FREE stock simulation platform where you can easily learn how to place trade orders (like market order, limit order, stop loss, etc), how to create a portfolio, how to create a watchlist and more. On registration, you'll get $100,000 as virtual cash which you can use to trade. You can also compete with thousands of Investopedia traders/players on the same platform.

The reason why I didn't place this platform in the top 3 is that you cannot trade in Indian stocks on the Investopedia stock simulator. Therefore, if you're looking to learn virtual stock trading in India, then it might not be a good option. However, if you are comfortable with trading in foreign stocks like Apple, Google, Amazon, etc, then feel free to check out this simulating platform.

CHAPTER TWENTY-FIVE

REAL MONEY WITH NO INVESTMENT

Tickertape ("TT") is a content and information platform for stocks, ETFs and other investment instruments, owned by Smallcase Technologies Private Limited (the "Company"). TT offers various services like stock screener - a tool to screen stocks based on various fundamental and technical parameters, Market Mood Index - sentiment indicator of Indian stock market, Learn - a portal to learn basic financial and economic terms etc ("Services").

The Company is a Research Analyst registered with SEBI under SEBI (Research Analyst) Regulations, 2014, having registration number - INH200005984. The Company is a private limited company, incorporated in the year 2015, having its registered office in Bangalore. The company builds technology platforms & investment products for retail investors to invest better in the Indian equities. You can visit the company website here – www.smallcase.com

DOWNLOAD THE TICKERTAPE APP OR LOGIN INTO WWW.TICKERTAPE.IN

YOU CAN EARN UPTO 3000RS DAILY WITH ABSOLUTELY NO INVESTMENT.

CHAPTER TWENTY-SIX

CITY MOUSE AND THE VILLAGE MOUSE

A country mouse invited his cousin who lived in the city to come visit him. The city mouse was so disappointed with the sparse meal which was nothing more than a few kernels of corn and a couple of dried berries.

"My poor cousin," said the city mouse, "you hardly have anything to eat! I do believe that an ant could eat better! Please do come to the city and visit me, and I will show you such rich feasts, readily available for the taking."

So the country mouse left with his city cousin who brought him to a splendid feast in the city's alley. The country mouse could not believe his eyes. He had never seen so much food in one place. There was bread, cheese, fruit, cereals, and grains of all sorts scattered about in a warm cozy portion of the alley.

The two mice settled down to eat their wonderful dinner, but before they barely took their first bites, a cat approached their dining area. The two mice scampered away and hid in a small uncomfortable hole until the cat left. Finally, it was quiet, and the unwelcome visitor went to prowl somewhere else. The two mice ventured out of the hole and resumed their abundant feast. Before they could get a proper taste in their mouth, another visitor intruded on their dinner, and the two little mice had to scuttle away quickly.

"Goodbye," said the country mouse, "You do, indeed, live in a plentiful city, but I am going home where I can enjoy my dinner in peace."

A modest life with peace and quiet is better than a richly one with danger and strife.

CHAPTER TWENTY-SEVEN

YOUTUBE CHANNEL GUIDE

Create Youtube Channel

You can start your youtube channel just by logging through your gmail account but that solely, will not give you any money. To make money, you must follow all the steps described under the heading **how to earn money from youtube** (below).

1. To start, open youtube.com with your Gmail account.
2. Click on the bar beside the Youtube logo on the left corner.
3. Click on My Channels from the drop down menu (as shown in the image above)
4. A box with heading 'Set up your channel on YouTube' will appear, with your name highlighted.
5. Update channel with your personal information.

Pro Tip

Create a custom YouTube URL instead of the default youtube URL to get organic search visibility.

By default, Youtube gives you a URL like this, www.youtube.com/user/abcdefd0h0d2r....... But you must create your channel's brand name url like www.youtube.com/user/CashOverflow.

Experts say this helps your channel to get visibility in search results. There are certain mandatory requirements for getting a custom URL though, but I believe you are highly dedicated to fulfill those requirements.

Check the requirements and the process of getting a **custom Youtube URL**.

If you haven't created your youtube channel till now, To help you please follow this guidelines

How to Start a YouTube Channel for Beginners

You can create youtube channel by following these easy steps

STEPS INVOLVED IN CREATING A CHANNEL:

Step #1. Creating YouTube Login

Step #2. Creating YouTube Channel

Step #3. Create Studio

Step #4. Upload Video

#1. Make Videos What You Like the Most

#2. Primary Focus Should be on the Content Quality, Rather Than Video Production Quality

#3. Start With Simple Editing Software

#4. Invest in the Essential Tools

#5. Consistency Matters the Most, Hence Post Videos Regularly

#6. Engage With Your Audience & Get Feedback

#1. Post Videos on Your Blog

#2. Share Videos With Your Email List

#3. Share Links With Friends

#4. Optimizing YouTube Channel for SEO

Step #1. Creating YouTube Login

You will require a google account for creating a YouTube channel. If you do not have a Google account then create one at Google.com.

If you already have a Google account, you can directly go to YouTube and click "sign-in" on the top right corner of the webpage.

Login using Google account that you would like to be associated with. On signing up you will get the following page.

Step #2. Creating YouTube Channel

Click on "Your Channel" from the dropdown (as shown in the red box above) to create a channel. The following page will open up. Click on "Create Channel".

Step #3. Create Studio

After channel creation, you have to create a studio. The 'Create Studio is in the dropdown from the sign-in menu as shown here;

Click on create studio for starting channel.

Step #4. Upload Video

The YouTube channel is now ready and you can start uploading your best videos.

How Many Views and Subscribers You Need to Make Money From Youtube in 2020

YouTube has changed the monetization policy by putting the following clause.

- Channels to have minimum 1000 subscribers
- The minimum time watched in last 1 year should be 4000 hours

That means YouTube also expects your 1000 subscribers to watch 4 hours of your videos on an average to complete 4000 hours. That won't be possible if they are not deeply engaged with your content.

The idea is to create quality content so that you could engage with the user base. Users want something contextually correlated with their needs, so if your content doesn't meet the need then the user will get disengaged. You have to match with the intent and purpose of the user.

The users would dis-engage with your YouTube channel if videos deviate too much from the core identity of your channel. Great content does not mean production quality, primarily great content means highly educative relevant content on niche topics.

Tips for Starting a YouTube Channel

#1. Make Videos What You Like the Most

Because this helps you in creating a quality content and keep the subscribers engaged.

#2. Primary Focus Should be on the Content Quality, Rather Than Video Production Quality

Because quality content will pull and engage users on the channel. If the content is relevant then users will revisit your channel again and again.

#3. Start With Simple Editing Software

You are still at the learning stage, so start small. There are free video editors like Filmora (both free & paid), iMovie, Windows Movie Maker and YouTube Video Editor, which you can use to create a quality video.

#4. Invest in the Essential Tools

Essential tools like Camera, Wireless Microphone, Tripod, Lighting and Video Editing Software help you create good quality videos.

#5. Consistency Matters the Most, Hence Post Videos Regularly

Consistency keeps the audience engaged and loyal. The users come frequently to your channel looking for relevant content. Users could share your video on their social networks if they find value.

#6. Engage With Your Audience & Get Feedback

Constructive feedback helps in building channels' credibility through mature engagement. Most importantly, this will help you in building a long-term relationship with subscribers.

How to Promote YouTube Channel in the Initial Days

#1. Post Videos on Your Blog

You can insert the videos in the relevant articles on your blog. This will help you to promote your videos in the starting stage of your youtube channel. You will get views and subscribers on your youtube channel through your blog post.

Videos in the blog article will also increase the session time, which would help in your blog SEO.

#2. Share Videos With Your Email List

If you already have an email list, then you can keep sharing your videos with your audience through emails.

Email marketing is an easy and effective way to increase the subscriber base in the early stage if you already have a strong email list.

#3. Share Links With Friends

Your friends on social media platforms could be a great asset in the promotion. You can request them personally to push the video in their own network to drive traffic.

Even this tactic would work if your content is engaging and high quality.

#4. Optimizing YouTube Channel for SEO

Optimizing for SEO helps in channel discovery as your videos start coming in organic search. There are several tools you can use to optimize for SEO purpose;

Tools

- **Tubebuddy** – This is a browser extension for YouTube, Tubebuddy video SEO can help with keyword rank tracker, search rankings and explorer, tags and even video A/B testing. All are very helpful in rankings boost and thereby promotion of the channel.
- **Vidiq** – help you leverage tools and strategy to master video marketing initiatives and grow a loyal audience of consumers. This can be done through Vidiq's creator solutions and brand solutions.

Things required to optimise are

- **Tags** – descriptive tags added to video will help people find your content easily.
- **Title** – is an important piece of metadata that summarizes the entire video. Well-written titles improve rankings and click through rates.
- **Description** – helps in understanding the context and the content of the video. Well optimized descriptions can lead to higher rankings and helping viewers understand and find your videos more easily.

The length of the video matters a lot because YouTube gives weightage to watch-time over the number of views. While starting, do not worry too much and just focus on creating the best possible video so that it could drive engagement.

Initially, YouTube allows 15 minutes of video uploads. Once the account gets verification you could get a video space of up to 20GB.

How to Start a YouTube Channel & Make Money

There are many ways to make money from youtube. Even you can discover your own new ways to monetize your youtube channel once you have built a audience.

But do not jump in the money-making race, instantly. Remember, the initial three phases are important. Start thinking of monetizing only when you have enough quality content and an engaging subscriber base.

Apply for YouTube Adsense when you have 1000 subscribers and 4000 hours of watch time.

Once you link Google Adsense to your YouTube account, you can get paid when someone clicks on an ad or watches your videos for at least 30 seconds.

But I do not consider adding ads on the channel as profitable because 1000 clicks will earn $10 to $15 commission. The amount will vary depending on the people and the geography from where they are clicking and what action they are taking.

This way making a decent profit would require millions of subscribers which can be a challenging task in the early days.

The other effective way you can try out is affiliate marketing. You can insert affiliate links of various partners, especially Amazon, in your videos where you are reviewing the product. The best way is to leave the link at the bottom of the video.

If you have a large subscriber base then you can target reviewing new companies and their products. This way you can help the new company increase visibility and can even charge a percentage of 10% to 20% of the sales happening through your channel.